Understanding Change

SpiritBuilt Leadership 7

Malcolm Webber

Published by:

Strategic Press
www.StrategicPress.org

Strategic Press is a division of Strategic Global Assistance, Inc.
www.sgai.org

513 S. Main St. Suite 2
Elkhart, IN 46516
U.S.A.

+1-844-532-3371 (LEADER-1)

ISBN 978-1-888810-01-1

All Scripture references are from the New International Version of the Bible, unless otherwise noted.

Printed in the United States of America

Table of Contents

Introduction

Leading change is one of the most difficult leadership responsibilities. It is also one of the most important. The world around us is constantly changing, and, to be effective in it, our organizations must change, too. Organizations that do not change rapidly become irrelevant and impotent. Moreover, to fully exploit the many opportunities that lie before us requires organizations that are nimble, quick and lively.

Change is necessary for two basic reasons:

1. To solve existing problems.
2. To move ahead into the opportunities God opens for us.

The top leadership team usually leads major change in an organization, but any member of the organization can initiate change or contribute to its success. This requires humility and perceptiveness in the leaders.

In a broad sense, what leaders do is stage continuous reformations. Leaders go for God's highest! They constantly challenge the status quo, and when they recognize new opportunities or see something that needs to be changed, they do something about it. Thus, to be effective, leaders must understand change.

It is our hope and prayer that this small booklet will help Christian leaders around the world to be more effective change agents for the glory of God.

Malcolm Webber, Ph.D.
Strategic Press
December, 2000

chapter 1

Resistance to Change

Most people prefer stability and predictability in their lives and ministries. Consequently, proposed change causes stress for most people. This is why when faced with changes to the status quo, people usually resist at first. Moreover, their resistance will often continue and sometimes increase, until they are able to recognize that the benefits of the proposed change outweigh the accompanying stress and potential pain.

Efforts to implement change are more likely to succeed if a leader understands the many possible reasons for resistance to change:

1. **Lack of trust.** Distrust of the people who propose change will cause resistance to it. Even when there is no obvious threat, a change may be resisted if people imagine there are hidden and ominous implications that will only later become apparent. Furthermore, mutual distrust may encourage a leader to be secretive about the reasons for change (and even about the change itself), thereby increasing suspicion and resistance.

2. **Perception that change is not necessary.** Without an obvious need for change, people will resist it. If the current way of doing things has been successful in the past, and there is no clear evidence of serious problems, people will resist change.

   When an organization has become very successful, its greatest strengths can become its greatest weaknesses by encouraging complacency and pride. The very best times can become the most dangerous. Fortified by a sense of invulnerability, the organization can become blind to its own need for significant reassessment and change.

> *You say, "I am rich; I have acquired wealth and do not need a thing." But you do not realize that you are wretched, pitiful, poor, blind and naked. (Rev. 3:17)*

Unfortunately, the signs of a developing problem are usually unclear in the early stages, and it is easy for people to ignore, discount or misinterpret them.

Furthermore, if the leadership has exaggerated how well the organization has been performing, then convincing people of the need for change will be even more difficult. Even when a problem is recognized, the usual response is to make incremental adjustments in the present strategy, rather than to do something entirely different.

3. **Perception that change is not possible.** Even when everyone acknowledges the problem, the proposed change will still be resisted if it seems unlikely to succeed; and making a change that is radically different from anything done previously will usually appear very difficult – if not impossible – to most people. Furthermore, the failure of earlier change attempts creates cynicism and makes people doubtful whether the next attempt will succeed either. With cynical people, leaders rarely achieve successful change.

4. **Economic threats.** Even if a change will obviously benefit the organization, it will likely be resisted by people who would suffer personal loss of income, benefits, job security or seniority. This is one of the major reasons why technological change is commonly resisted, in spite of its frequently obvious benefits. Moreover, prior downsizing and layoffs raise anxiety and increase resistance to new proposals, regardless of the actual threat.

5. **Relatively high costs.** All change involves some cost. Familiar routines must be changed, creating inconveniences and requiring more effort. Certain freedoms may be lost. Resources are necessary to implement change, and resources already invested in doing things the traditional way will be lost. Moreover, performance invariably suffers during the transition period as the new ways are learned and procedures debugged. Consequently, if it is not possible to accurately estimate these costs in relation to the benefits of the proposed change, there will be resistance.

6. **Fear of personal failure.** Some changes make expertise obsolete and require learning new ways of doing things. Many people will be reluctant to trade knowledge and skills they have mastered for new ones that may be too difficult to learn. Thus, proposed change will be more acceptable if it includes ample provision for training people in the new ways of doing things.

7. **Loss of status or power.** Major organizational changes invariably result in some shift of power and status for certain individuals and groups. New strategies often require expertise that is not possessed by some of the people currently enjoying high status as problem solvers. Those who are threatened with a loss of status and power will frequently oppose the change – even when it is obviously beneficial for the organization.

8. **Threats to values and ideals.** Threats to a person's values will arouse strong emotions that fuel resistance to change. Moreover, if the values are embedded in a strong organizational culture, then resistance will be widespread and not isolated.

9. **Resentment of interference.** Most people do not want to be controlled by others, and attempts to manipulate them or force change will elicit resentment and hostility. Unless people acknowledge the need for change and perceive they have a choice in determining how to change, they will resist it.

The Importance of Working with Resistance

Leaders must develop the proper attitude toward resistance to change and recognize that it is not necessarily the simple result of ignorance, inflexibility, weakness of character, or rebellion. It can be the normal defensive response of people who want to protect what they know and possess, as well as their own sense of purpose.

Indeed, sometimes the voice of resistance can serve as a signal that there are ways in which the change effort should be modified or improved. In this way, listening to those who initially resist can prevent us from taking untimely or foolish actions.

Rather than viewing resistance as an obstacle to beat down or circumvent, it is frequently more realistic and advantageous to see it as intellectual and emotional energy that can be redirected to improve change, once the opponents have been converted to supporters.

Consequently, rather than launching into lengthy self-justifications at the first sign of resistance, leaders should listen carefully, actively seeking out people's thoughts and reactions to the proposed changes.

The more that people are provided the opportunity to give input into the change process, the more they will be on board.

One of the leader's primary instruments of change is prayer that God will open the hearts of the people to embrace His purposes. We must recognize that people are not the enemies – Satan is the enemy.

> *Finally, be strong in the Lord and in his mighty power. Put on the full armor of God so that you can take your stand against the devil's schemes. For our struggle is not against flesh and blood, but against the rulers, against the authorities, against the powers of this dark world and against the spiritual forces of evil in the heavenly realms. (Eph. 6:10-12)*

As a servant of God, the Christian leader must be gentle and gracious toward those who oppose him, even when they are obviously wrong.

> *And the Lord's servant must not quarrel; instead, he must be kind to everyone, able to teach, not resentful. Those who oppose him he must gently instruct, in the hope that God will grant them repentance leading them to a knowledge of the truth, (2 Tim. 2:24-25)*

Showing respect toward those who resist builds stronger relationships, not only improving the change at hand by putting the leader in a place where he can hear ideas for improvement of his proposal, but also providing a stronger relational base for future changes.

Furthermore, leaders should recognize that they have already worked through the personal trauma and pain of the proposed change and its implications long before they even initially present it to their constituents. Consequently, it is sometimes easy for leaders to "jump to beginnings." Of course, this is never so easy for others who have not wrestled with the idea for as long and who are not personally as inclined to change in the first place. "Jumping to beginnings" is a temptation leaders must resist.

Finally, leaders must realize that, just as it takes miles to turn a large ship at sea, it often takes years to implement significant change in a large organization. Dramatic moments of "revolutionary" transformation are only a small part of it. Organizational change is longer and subtler than can be managed by a single leader. It is generated from the insights of many people working to improve the whole, and it accumulates over long periods. To lead change effectively, leaders must be committed to the long haul; God is!

> *being confident of this, that he who began a good work in you will carry it on to completion until the day of Christ Jesus. (Phil. 1:6)*

chapter 2

The Change Process

Leaders lead their constituents somewhere different from where they are already. Thus, the essence of leadership is change. Consequently, leaders must understand the change process and how change is achieved.

There is a typical pattern of events that occur from the beginning of a change to the end. Kurt Lewin, a researcher and social psychologist, divided the change process into three distinct phases: unfreezing, changing and refreezing.

1. **Unfreezing phase.** People come to realize that the old ways of doing things are no longer appropriate and that change is needed. This recognition may occur as a result of an obvious crisis or from the leaders' efforts to describe threats or opportunities not yet apparent to most people in the organization. An organizational "catharsis" of some kind is often necessary before the shell of complacency and self-righteousness is broken open and prejudices against major change removed.

2. **Changing phase.** People look for new ways of doing things and select an appropriate and promising approach.

3. **Refreezing phase.** The new approach is implemented and it becomes established.

All three phases are necessary for successful change. Moving too quickly through the stages can endanger the success of a change effort. If a leader attempts to move directly to the changing phase without first unfreezing the attitudes of his constituents, he is likely to meet with apathy at best and strong, organized resistance at worst.

Moreover, a lack of prayer, systematic diagnosis and problem solving in the changing phase will result in a weak change plan.

Finally, a lack of attention to consensus building and maintenance of enthusiasm in the third stage may result in the change being reversed soon after it is implemented.

This metaphor of unfreezing, changing and refreezing is useful in that it illuminates the distinct phases of the change process. Nevertheless, one should not overlook the fact that the status quo is not a static affair (as the image of "freezing" may lead us to believe) but a living and dynamic process. The status quo in an organization is "quasi-stationary" – like a river that continuously moves but still keeps a recognizable form. In leading change, the organizational structures, the people themselves and the outside world all need to be considered in their complex and dynamic interplay with each other.

How Change is Achieved

Change is achieved by two types of fundamental actions:

1. **Increasing the driving forces toward change.** For example, by setting forth vision or by increasing incentives, etc.

2. **Reducing the restraining forces that create resistance to change.** For example, by reducing fear of failure or economic loss, or by converting or removing opponents, etc.

If the restraining forces are weak, it may be sufficient merely to increase the positive, driving forces. However, when restraining forces are strong, a dual approach is usually best. Unless restraining forces can be reduced, an increase in driving forces will create an intense conflict over the change, and continuing resistance will make it more difficult to complete the unfreezing phase.

How People React To Change

To successfully lead organizational change, leaders must understand how people react to change.

People react to major organizational change in a manner similar to how they react to sudden traumatic events such as the death of a loved one, the breakup of a marriage, or a natural disaster that destroys one's home. The reaction pattern has four stages:

1. **Denial.** The initial reaction is to deny that change will be necessary. "This isn't happening" or "It's just a temporary setback."

2. **Anger.** The next stage is to get angry and look for someone to blame. At the same time, people stubbornly resist giving up accustomed ways of doing things.

3. **Mourning.** In this stage, people stop denying that change is inevitable, acknowledge what has been lost, and mourn it.

4. **Adaptation.** The final stage is to accept the need to change and get on with life.

The duration and severity of each type of reaction can vary greatly, and some people get stuck in an intermediate stage. Leaders must understand these stages and learn to be patient and helpful. Many people need help to overcome denial, conquer their anger, mourn without becoming depressed, and have optimism about adjusting successfully.

How People Are Affected by Repeated, Traumatic Change

People react in different ways to repeated, traumatic change. Many people are hurt by change. This leaves them less resilient and more vulnerable to damage by subsequent change. Others are "inoculated" by repeated changes and become better prepared to change again without having such an intense or prolonged period of adjustment.

Christian leaders must know their people, pray for them and with them, and seek to lead change in a manner that is healthy and beneficial. Organizational change should not hurt the people it was intended to serve. We will deal with the relationship of change to stress in a later chapter.

The Change Strategy

There are two basic ways to introduce change in an organization: change people or change roles. Leaders must understand these two dimensions of change.

1. **Change people.** This approach assumes that new attitudes or skills will cause behavior to change. Skills can be changed with training programs, and attitudes can be changed by persuasive appeals or by team building interventions. Prayer, of course, is the Christian leader's most potent way to bring change in people's hearts when that change is in line with God's will. "Converts" become change agents themselves and transmit the vision to other people in the organization.

2. **Change roles.** This approach assumes that when new roles require people to act in a different way, they will change their attitudes to be consistent with their new behavior. Roles can be changed by redesigning jobs to include different activities and responsibilities, by reorganizing the workflow, by modifying authority relationships, and by changing the criteria and procedures for the evaluation of work.

Either approach can succeed or fail depending on how it is implemented, as well as the circumstances surrounding it. Often the best strategy will be to use them together in a mutually supportive way, making efforts to change attitudes and skills to support new roles. This will minimize resistance and give change the best chance of success.

Using Someone Else's Change Strategy?

There are many generic change strategies for either attitude change or role change. In the business world, some examples include downsizing, delayering, self-managed teams, quality circles and incentive plans. Popular strategies come and go in every organizational context.

However, a common mistake is for a leader to implement one of these change strategies without a careful and prayerful diagnosis of the particular problems and opportunities facing his own organization. A single generic strategy is not likely to solve an organization's problems by itself, and it may make them worse.

Before initiating major changes, leaders must be clear about the nature of the problem or the opportunity and the objectives of the intended change.

Just as in the treatment of a physical illness, the first step is a careful diagnosis to determine what is wrong with the patient. The organizational diagnosis can be conducted by the top leadership team, by outside consultants, or by a team composed of representatives of the various key stakeholders in the organization. To succeed, the procedure must be submitted to the will and purposes of God, and it must be bathed in prayer.

After the diagnosis is completed, an appropriate change strategy can then be prayerfully designed with complementary changes in roles and people.

chapter 3

A Model of Planned Change

Large-scale change in an organization involves a process of experimentation and learning. It is impossible to anticipate all the possible problems or to prepare detailed plans for how to carry out all aspects of the change. In fact, contrary to common assumptions, the process of change in an organization is not always initiated by top management, and they may not even become involved until the process is well underway.

The essential role of leadership is to formulate an integrating vision and general strategy, build a coalition of supporters who endorse the strategy, then guide and coordinate the process by which the strategy will be implemented. Rather than specifying exact and detailed guidelines for change at all levels of the organization, it is much better to encourage middle- and lower-level managers to change their own units in a way that is consistent with the overall vision and strategy.

The leaders should provide encouragement, support, suggestions, and the necessary resources to facilitate change, but should not try to dictate exactly how to do it.

The Eight-Stage Model of Planned Organizational Change

Successful implementation of change requires a wide range of leadership behaviors that involve both organizational actions and people-oriented actions. In *Leading Change,* John Kotter presents an eight-stage model of planned change. This model includes both kinds of actions, and to

1. Establish a sense of urgency

2. Create a guiding coalition

3. Develop a compelling vision and strategy

4. Communicate the change vision widely

5. Empower constituents for broad-based action on the vision

6. Generate short-term wins

7. Consolidate gains and produce more change

8. Anchor new approaches in the organizational culture

successfully implement change, leaders must pay careful attention to each stage. Skipping stages or making critical mistakes at any stage can cause the change process to fail.

These are the eight broad stages:

We will now look at each stage in detail.

1. ESTABLISH A SENSE OF URGENCY.

Crises or threats will quickly thaw resistance to change. However, unless there is already an obvious crisis, most members of an organization are unlikely to comprehend the need for major change, and they will doubt whether the change is really worth the pain necessary to accomplish it.

Therefore, leaders must identify actual crises, potential crises as well as significant opportunities, and then find ways to communicate the information broadly and convincingly.

Establishing a sense of urgency is crucial to gaining needed cooperation. If urgency is low and complacency high, transformations usually go nowhere.

There are many sources of organizational complacency, all of which help maintain the status quo:

1. A lack of prayer and seeking God for His highest purposes to be accomplished by the organization. If we were truly seeking God's will, we would realize how far short we fall.
2. No major and highly visible crisis. "Church is comfortable, no divisions recently, the bills are paid; we're okay, aren't we?"
3. Success. Too many visible resources. "We're growing; why change now?" For many organizations, their time of greatest success becomes the time of their initial declension.
4. Low overall performance standards. Several years ago, two house church movements in China set a combined goal of

leading 40 million people to the Lord in a two month period. This would be accomplished by each leader leading 5 people to the Lord and each believer leading 3 people to the Lord in that time period. In the United States, many churches are thrilled to see a single person saved per year!

5. Organizational structures that focus constituents on narrow functional goals, instead of broad organizational performance. Too absorbed with narrow "busy" details, we lose the big picture of our actual state.

6. Internal measurement systems that focus on the wrong performance indexes. "Are the church's small groups following everything in the agendas they are given?" versus "Are they winning souls?"

7. A lack of sufficient performance feedback from external sources. Self-absorbed and egocentric, we are often too insulated from our environments to get any legitimate feedback regarding our real performance. Church may look pretty on Sunday, but what are we really accomplishing?

8. A kill-the-messenger-of-bad-news, low-candor, low-confrontation culture. "Quiet! Don't rock the boat! You may make people feel bad!"

9. Too much "happy talk" from senior leaders. We are particularly guilty of this in the church: always trying to make people feel better than how they really should be feeling.

10. Human nature, with its capacity for denial, especially if people are already busy or stressed.

To break complacency's power, there are a number of ways to raise a sense of urgency:

1. Pray for the power of the Holy Spirit to convict the people of their complacency in the face of the organization's real problems and opportunities.

2. Allow errors to occur instead of correcting them at the last minute.

3. Eliminate obvious examples of excess. "If the pastor drives a

BMW, why should I sacrifice for missions?"

4. Set goals so high that they can not be reached by conducting business as usual. God has called us to change the world!

5. Stop measuring performance based only on narrow functional goals and, instead, hold people accountable for the broad performance of the organization. What are we really accomplishing?

6. Inform the constituents about the real performance of the organization, especially its weaknesses.

7. Insist that everyone in the organization is personally exposed to the real problems the organization faces. Ultimately, we're all responsible for the success or failure of our organizations.

8. Bring outsiders in to force more relevant data and honest discussion into leadership meetings. Counteract insider myopia with external data. "You say, 'I am rich; I have acquired wealth and do not need a thing.' But you do not realize that you are wretched, pitiful, poor, blind and naked." (Rev. 3:17)

9. Be more honest when discussing the organization's problems with its constituents. Let's be honest for a change, instead of always trying to be positive. Eliminate leadership "happy talk"!

10. Bombard people with information on future opportunities and possibilities, on the rewards of fulfilling those possibilities, and on the organization's current inability to pursue those opportunities. We may be surprised by how they rise to the challenge!

2. CREATE A GUIDING COALITION.

It is dangerous to think that a single leader can pull off major organizational change single-handed. The task of persuading people to support major change is never easy, and it is too big a job for a single leader to accomplish alone. Successful change in an organization requires cooperative effort by people who have the power to facilitate or block change.

The leaders must build a team of "change supporters" both inside and outside the organization. These should come not only from the top leadership, but also from among middle and lower levels of management. This team must share the commitment to the need and possibilities for organizational transformation, and they will guide the change process.

Eight key characteristics are essential to effective guiding coalitions:

1. Prayer. The team that prays together will not only have a clearer understanding of the nature and process of the change, but will also carry a stronger spiritual anointing to facilitate it.
2. Submission to the will of God. The leaders must humbly and genuinely submit themselves to God's will for the organization. It is not enough merely to ask God to bless our proposed changes; we must first be sure they are His proposals!
3. Key leaders. The key players in the organization need to be on board. Sometimes people will work to block change simply because they were not a part of the original guiding coalition.

   There is no better way to minimize resistance to change than to involve those responsible for implementing it and those affected by it. If there is no involvement early on in the planning, during the implementation and throughout perpetuation, the change effort will fail. When people know that they are valued participants in planning and implementing the change, they are more likely to be motivated toward successful completion. Here are two simple principles to follow when building an effective change team:

   - It is wise to err on the side of involving more people rather than fewer. If there is a question as to whether or not a certain person's support will be needed, include them.
   - Ensure that people from all levels of the organization are involved in planning the change process. This means involving the people who will most be affected by the proposed change. More than anyone else, they will make the change process succeed or fail.

4. Expertise. No one individual has sufficient information to make all the major decisions. Represented in the team should be all the various points of view relevant to the situation – in terms of discipline, experience, age, nationality, gender, etc.
5. Credibility. Again, no single individual has sufficient credibility to convince all the constituents to implement the decisions. Team members must possess good reputations and be trusted and taken seriously across the organization.
6. Leadership. The team must include enough proven leaders to be able to drive the change process. Of course, management skills are also needed on the team.
7. Integrity. Personal problems that can be ignored during easy times can cause serious trouble in harder, faster-moving times. People with large egos who do not realize their own weaknesses and limitations or appreciate the strengths of others, and also people who create mistrust by playing people against each other should not be considered for such a team.
8. Trust. When people trust each other, creating a common goal and strategy becomes possible. Frequent and open communication helps build this necessary trust; and to maintain it, rumors that might erode goodwill between team members must be confronted immediately and candidly.

3. DEVELOP A COMPELLING VISION AND STRATEGY.

Leaders are responsible for formulating and articulating a compelling vision that will guide the change effort and for developing the strategies for achieving that vision. A "picture" of a highly desirable future motivates people to change.

A good vision serves three important purposes:

1. By clarifying the general direction for change, it simplifies hundreds of more detailed decisions. One simple question – is

this in line with the vision? – can eliminate much discussion. Moreover, all available people and resources can be mobilized in the same direction.

2. It motivates people to take action in the right direction, even if the first steps require sacrifice and are personally painful.
3. It helps align and coordinate the actions of many different people in a fast and efficient way. With clarity of vision, constituents can determine what to do for themselves without constantly checking with their superiors or peers.

An effective vision has six characteristics. It is:

1. Imaginable. It conveys a picture of what the future could look like. The vision must be ambitious enough to force people out of their comfort zones. The God we serve created the universe; He can do great things!
2. Desirable. It appeals to the long-term interests of most of the organization's stakeholders. In contrast, poor visions tend to ignore the legitimate interests of some groups or to exploit other groups.
3. Realistic. Good visions are not "pie-in-the-sky" fantasies with no chance of realization. Here are several guidelines for developing a realistic vision:
    - Christian leaders must be careful not to let a cavalier "all things are possible with God" attitude to substitute for a legitimate vision that is, at once, faith-filled yet realistic. If the vision is not realistic or practical, it will fail, creating organizational cynicism and causing future change efforts to be derailed before they even begin.
    - Good visions will take advantage of fundamental trends.
    - To be realistic, the vision should be linked to the core competencies of the organization.
4. Focused. Good visions are clear enough to motivate action. They should not be vague or ambiguous.
5. Flexible. Good visions must be flexible enough to allow initiative. Bad visions are sometimes too specific or do not

allow for modification. As the change proceeds, the vision itself will often change! So it must be flexible to begin with.

6. Communicable. An effective vision can be explained successfully within five minutes. Unintelligible visions are ineffective. The trumpet must sound a clear and compelling call.

In creating an effective vision, there are certain steps that can profitably be followed:

1. First idea. The process often starts with an initial statement from a single individual, reflecting his or her dreams as well as real organizational needs or opportunities.

2. Role of the guiding coalition. The first idea is then modified over time by the guiding coalition or by another larger group of stakeholders. Teamwork is vital to this process.

3. Roles of the head and the heart. Both analytic thinking and a lot of prayerful "dreaming" are essential throughout the activity. Think, dream, be creative! You may be stuck in a rut, but God is not. He is the ultimate Creator of new opportunities!

4. Stay in prayer and in the Word of God. Discerning the will of God must be the central theme in the process. He will bless His vision; He may or may not bless yours!

5. Role of relevant elements in the old ideology. Even when radical change is necessary in an organization, some elements in the current way may be worthy of preservation. Sometimes traditional values that were subverted or ignored will serve as the basis for the new (albeit old) vision. On other occasions, it might be wise to include benign older elements rather than risk alienating key people who value those elements.

6. Messiness of the process. Vision creation is usually a process of two steps forward and one step back, movement to the left and then to the right.

7. Time frame. Vision is never created in a single sitting. It takes months, sometimes years to form a powerful vision.

8. End product. A good vision is never finished but is continually assessed and refined to reflect the current understanding of God's perfect will for the organization.

4. COMMUNICATE THE CHANGE VISION WIDELY.

The real transforming power of vision is unleashed when most of an organization's constituents share a common understanding of its goals and direction. Therefore, leaders must use every means possible to communicate widely the vision and strategy. Change is impossible unless a majority of people in the organization are involved and willing to help, often to the point of personal sacrifice. Consequently, effective communication will frequently make the difference between success and failure.

The key elements in the effective communication of vision are:

1. Simplicity. All profession-specific jargon must be eliminated. Simple, concise and clear communication is most potent.
2. Passion. If the leaders who are promoting the change do not look as if they either believe it themselves or are willing to sacrifice for its achievement, how can they expect the people to embrace it?
3. Metaphor, analogy and example. Vision should be imaginative. Colorful and picturesque language can communicate complex ideas quickly, effectively and memorably. Symbols can be easily understood and remembered. Rather than relying on complicated and abstract descriptions, wise leaders will follow the extensive examples of Jesus and the biblical writers and develop symbols that express the heart of their vision.
4. Multiple forums. Vision is usually communicated most effectively when many different vehicles are used: large group meetings, small group discussions, memos, brochures, flyers, emails, posters, informal one-on-one talks. When the same message comes at people from many different directions, it stands a better chance of being heard and remembered, on both intellectual and emotional levels.

5. Repetition. People's minds are so cluttered that any communication has to fight hundreds of other ideas for attention. One time is never enough. Leaders should communicate about change at least 10 times more than they think necessary.
6. Leadership by example. When the leaders act out the vision, many troublesome questions about credibility tend to evaporate. On the other hand, nothing undermines the communication of a change vision more than behaviors on the parts of key players that appear to be inconsistent with the vision.
7. Explanation of seeming inconsistencies. If mixed signals cannot be eliminated, they should be explained, simply and honestly.
8. Listen and be listened to. The communication of vision is not a one-way broadcast. In successful change efforts, communication always becomes two-way.

Leaders should design mechanisms that provide ongoing feedback from constituents throughout the change effort. Involved people can be effective barometers of what is working well and what is not working well. They should be asked to suggest improvements. Any errors that are exposed in the change process should be eliminated.

Moreover, people will usually embrace a new vision only after wrestling with it. Wrestling means asking questions, challenging, arguing and praying together. Of course, in this dialogue the leaders may discover that their vision needs to be adjusted or even entirely reformulated. However, in the end, swallowing their pride and reworking the vision is far more productive than charging off in the wrong direction – or in a direction others will not follow.

5. EMPOWER CONSTITUENTS FOR BROAD-BASED ACTION ON THE VISION.

Major organizational change rarely happens unless many people assist. However, constituents will not help, or cannot help, if they feel powerless. Consequently, leaders must empower their constituents if they are serious about change. This means getting rid of obstacles to change, which may require revising systems, structures or procedures that hinder or undermine the change effort. People can be empowered with knowledge, resources and discretion to make things happen. Leaders can also encourage and reward risk-taking and nontraditional ideas and actions.

To empower people to effect change, leaders should:

1. Communicate a rational and clear vision to constituents. If constituents have a shared sense of purpose, it is easier to initiate actions to achieve that purpose.
2. Once constituents are "on board" with the vision, they should be given the authority to move in the new direction as they see best. Responsibility without authority causes frustration.
3. Make organizational structures compatible with the vision. This includes aligning information and personnel systems to the vision. Unaligned structures and systems block needed action.
4. Provide the training that constituents need. Without the right skills and attitudes, people feel disempowered.
5. Confront supervisors who undercut needed change. Nothing disempowers people the way a negative boss can.

6. GENERATE SHORT-TERM WINS.

Leaders plan for visible performance improvements, enable them to happen, and celebrate constituents who were involved in the improvements. Major change takes time, and a transformation effort loses momentum if there are no short-term accomplishments that people can recognize and celebrate. Short-term wins boost the credibility of the process and renew the commitment and enthusiasm of constituents.

A good short-term win has at least three characteristics:

1. It is visible; large numbers of people can see for themselves that the result is real and not just hype.
2. It is clear and unambiguous, so there can be little argument about it.
3. It is clearly related to the overall change effort.

Furthermore, short-term wins help long-term transformation in the following ways:

1. They provide evidence that sacrifices are worth it. Wins greatly help justify the short-term costs involved.
2. They reward change agents with affirmation. After a lot of hard work, positive feedback builds morale and motivation.
3. They help fine-tune vision and strategies. Short-term wins give the guiding coalition concrete data on the viability of their plans.
4. They undermine cynics and self-serving resisters. Clear wins make it difficult for people to block needed change.
5. They keep stakeholders on board, by providing evidence that the transformation is on track.
6. They build momentum. Wins turn previously neutral people into supporters and reluctant supporters into active helpers.

7. CONSOLIDATE GAINS AND PRODUCE MORE CHANGE.

Leaders should build on the credibility achieved by short-term wins to consolidate improvements, tackle bigger problems and create greater change. They should resist the inclination to let up after a short-term win, knowing that if they let up before the job is done, critical momentum can be lost and regression may follow. After a measure of success, it is a subtle temptation for people to take a "deserved rest." However, until change processes completely permeate the organization's culture, they can be fragile and easily undone. Once regression begins, rebuilding momentum can be a daunting task, similar to asking people to throw their bodies in front of a huge boulder that has already begun to roll back down the hill.

People look to their leaders for signs of continued commitment to the change objectives and vision. Any indication that the change is no longer viewed as important or feasible may have ripple effects that undermine the change effort. Supporters will be lost and opponents encouraged to increase overt resistance.

Therefore, instead of "taking a breather," leaders should engage remaining systems, structures and policies that do not fit the vision. They should hire, promote and develop constituents who can implement the vision for change, and they should revitalize the process with a new round of projects, themes or change agents.

Great leaders are willing to think long term and to stay the course to accomplish the long-term goals. So, instead of declaring victory and giving up after a short-term win, they will launch a dozen new change projects, taking the time to ensure that all the new practices are firmly grounded in the organization's culture.

8. ANCHOR NEW APPROACHES IN THE ORGANIZATIONAL CULTURE.

Organizational culture is the pattern of attitudes, beliefs and values shared by the organization's members, which produces norms that shape the behavior of individuals and groups in the organization. Like national culture, organizational culture is usually rooted in deeply held values and is often very difficult to change.

It is in the culture that the changes must be made to stick. The new approaches must be institutionalized in the organizational culture. Old habits, values, traditions and mind-sets must be permanently replaced. New values and beliefs must be instilled in the culture so that constituents view the changes not as something new but as a normal and integral part of how the organization functions.

Change that is anchored in an organizational culture:

1. Comes last, not first. Most alterations in norms and shared values come at the end of the transformation process. Thus, change strategies that start with "changing the culture" as their first step are probably doomed to failure.
2. Must be carefully monitored for results. New approaches usually sink into a culture only after it is clear that they work and are superior to old values and methods.
3. Must be seen through to completion. When people within the organization begin to suspect that senior leaders are more interested in starting new programs than in the follow-through necessary to complete them, they will lose the sense of urgency and commitment to the initiatives and be more skeptical about any future change efforts.
4. Requires a lot of talk. Without repeated verbal instruction and support, people are often reluctant to embrace new practices, or even to admit their validity.
5. May involve turnover of personnel. Sometimes the only way to change a culture is to change key people. This makes decisions on succession crucial. If promotion processes are not changed to be compatible with the new practices, the old culture will reassert itself. A means must be developed to ensure leadership development and succession so that the new values and behaviors are carried forward to the next generation of leadership. Or, at least, until they need to be changed again!

chapter 4

Helping People Through Change

Even when a major change is clearly necessary and beneficial, it is stressful and painful for people. Change causes adjustment, discomfort, disruption and dislocation. A vital part of the process of implementing change involves encouraging people. Even those who are initially excited about a change will need continued support as the inevitable difficulties and failures occur. It is the leader's responsibility to:

1. **Prepare people to adjust to change.** Change requires difficult adjustments by the people who are most affected. If people are unable to handle the stress of change, they may become depressed or mutinous. Alternating successes and failures give even the most optimistic change agents the feeling that they are on an emotional roller coaster. Uncertainty about progress and the repeated discovery of new obstacles increase fatigue and frustration.

   All these negative aspects of change are easier to cope with if the people know in advance what to expect and how to deal with it. God tells His children in advance about the trials and difficulties that await them:

   > *They preached the good news in that city and won a large number of disciples. Then they returned to Lystra, Iconium and Antioch, strengthening the disciples and encouraging them to remain true to the faith. "We must go through many hardships to enter the kingdom of God," they said. (Acts 14:21-22; cf. John 16:13; Acts 9:16; etc.)*

It is far better to be realistic about the necessary adjustments and pain than to present the upcoming change as a cure-all with no costs or problems. One strategy is to find another organization that has implemented similar change and have someone from it share about their experiences and what they did to get through their change successfully.

2. **Help people deal with the loss that change brings.** When significant changes occur, some people experience personal pain at the loss of familiar things to which they had become attached. This trauma may be experienced whether the change involves new strategies and programs, new equipment and work procedures, new facilities, new management practices, or new leaders. Leaders can help their people by allowing them to verbalize their sense of loss and grief, and then gently pointing them to the benefits of the change and the bright new future before them. Leaders should also pray for and with their constituents for the grace of God to help them make the transition.

3. **Keep people informed about the progress of change.** In a time of stress and anxiety, such as is produced by major change, people look to their leaders to explain what is happening and to keep them informed. People will be more optimistic and enthusiastic if they know the change is progressing successfully. Leaders should frequently communicate what steps have been initiated, what changes have been completed and what resulting improvements have occurred. Successes should be celebrated and people recognized for their contributions and achievements. When obstacles are encountered, the leaders should explain what they are and what will be done about them. If the plan for change must be revised, leaders should explain why it was necessary. Otherwise, people may interpret revisions as a sign of faltering commitment or impending disaster.

4. **Encourage people to continue to look to the Lord.** God holds the future in His hands, and if the change is in line with His will and purposes, He will see the organization through. God is faithful.

Being confident of this, that he who began a good work in you will carry it on to completion until the day of Christ Jesus." (Phil. 1:6)

...And surely I am with you always, to the very end of the age. (Matt. 28:20)

chapter 5

How People Adopt Change

People in an organization do not embrace change at the same time. According to Everett Rogers' classic book, *Diffusion of Innovations*, people adopt "innovations" according to the various stages of a normal, bell-shaped curve (see chart). Significantly, these five kinds of people can be found at any level in the organization.

It should be noted that Rogers' model is a generalization, setting forth the general idea of categories of adopter types. It will rarely be exactly the same in all situations.

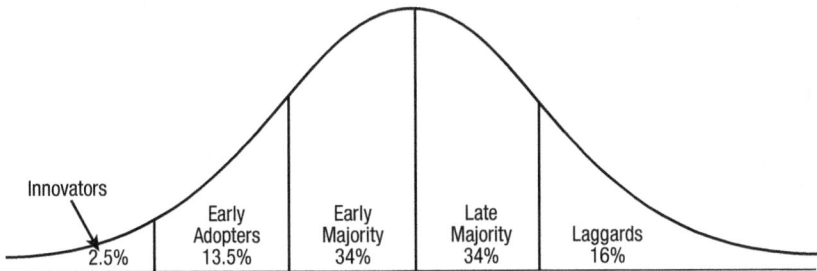

| Innovators 2.5% | Early Adopters 13.5% | Early Majority 34% | Late Majority 34% | Laggards 16% |

The "innovators" are the first 2.5% of the people in the organization to adopt an innovation. The next 13.5% to adopt the new idea are the "early adopters." The next 34% of the adopters are called the "early majority." The "late majority" is the next 34% to embrace the innovation, and the last 16% to adopt are called "laggards." It is very important that leaders, in bringing organizational change, focus their time and energy appropriately with each particular group of people.

The Five Categories

Innovators: These people have a great, almost obsessive, interest in new ideas. They desire the rash, the daring and the risky. Their thirst for new ideas leads them to form networks beyond the confines of the local circles. They can cope with a high degree of uncertainty regarding the success of a new idea and are willing to accept occasional setbacks. Many times they will not bother to perfect the innovation before moving on to the next one. Innovators may not be respected by the other members of the organization and might be seen as "radicals"; however, they are important to watch since they are frequently the gatekeepers in the flow of new ideas into the organization from outside its paradigmatic boundaries.

Early Adopters: These are the opinion leaders in the organization, and they represent the main people that the leader should identify and enlist in the change process. The early adopters are the role models for others who respect them for their judicious "innovation-decisions." Potential adopters look up to them for advice and information about the change because they are not too far ahead of the other members of the organization, in contrast with the innovators who are usually seen as being too far out ahead. Early adopters decrease uncertainty about a new idea by adopting it and then sharing their evaluation of the idea with their peers through personal relationships. This assists leaders in bringing organizational change.

Early Majority: Comprising about one-third of the people, the early majority adopt new ideas just before the average member of the organization. They are not opinion leaders, but they do interact frequently with their peers. They make decisions slowly, and they carefully analyze the pros and cons of a new idea before adopting it. They follow with deliberate willingness in embracing change but seldom lead.

Late Majority: The late majority adopt innovations just after the average member of the organization. Skeptical and cautious, they do not adopt until most others have done so and only then in response to the pressure of their peers and the new organizational norms.

Laggards: The last in the organization to embrace change, laggards possess almost no opinion leadership. Typically, they are somewhat isolated in their relational networks, interacting primarily with others who have relatively traditional values. They usually make decisions in terms of what has been done previously and are typically suspicious of change and change agents.

Characteristics of the Five Categories

According to Rogers, the five types of adopters vary in their socioeconomic characteristics, their personalities and their communication behavior. Again it should be noted that these are generalizations and will not be true in every situation.

SOCIOECONOMIC CHARACTERISTICS:

- Earlier adopters are not different from later adopters in age. The research shows no consistent relationship between age and innovativeness.
- Earlier adopters have more years of formal education than later adopters.
- Earlier adopters have higher social status (as indicated by income, occupational prestige, etc.) than later adopters.
- Earlier adopters have a greater degree of upward social mobility than later adopters. Moreover, they are on the move in the direction of still higher levels of social status. Sometimes they may use the adoption of change as one means of getting there.

PERSONALITY VARIABLES:

- Earlier adopters have greater empathy (the ability to project oneself into another person's situation) than later adopters. This ability is an important quality for an innovator, who must be imaginative and able to think outside of his own "box."

- Earlier adopters may be less dogmatic than later adopters. A highly dogmatic person will often not welcome new ideas but instead cling to the past.
- Earlier adopters have a greater ability to deal with abstractions than do later adopters. Innovators must be able to adopt a new idea largely on the basis of theoretical or creative abstractions. Later adopters, however, can observe the concrete realities of the new innovation when it is underway.
- Earlier adopters have a more favorable attitude toward change than later adopters.
- Earlier adopters are better able to cope with uncertainty and risk than later adopters.
- Earlier adopters have a more favorable attitude toward technology than later adopters.
- Earlier adopters are less fatalistic than later adopters. A person is more likely to adopt an innovation if he believes that his choices will make a genuine difference.
- Earlier adopters have higher aspirations (for formal education, occupations, etc.) than later adopters.

COMMUNICATION BEHAVIOR:

- Earlier adopters have more social participation than later adopters. They have active relationships with more people.
- Earlier adopters network more with others about ideas and practices than do later adopters.
- Earlier adopters are more likely to relate to people outside the boundaries of their "system" than are later adopters. This allows them to bring in more ideas from the "outside."
- Earlier adopters have more personal contact with the change agents than later adopters.
- Earlier adopters have greater exposure to mass media communication channels than later adopters.
- Earlier adopters seek information about innovations more actively than later adopters.
- Earlier adopters have a higher degree of opinion leadership

than later adopters. Others are more likely to look to them for leadership.

Understanding these differences can help leaders to recognize the various types of people and to develop different approaches for each adopter category.

chapter 6

Change and Stress

Stress is directly related to change. Of course, not all stress is bad. Life without stress would be life without change, which would be life without growth, which would be life without life! Without at least some change and stress, we will go nowhere.

On the other hand, if there is too much change and stress, things start to break down. High levels of stress contribute to a myriad of physical, emotional, spiritual and relational problems. Moreover, when stress is pushed to the extremes, burnout occurs. If you take a small sapling and bend it over, it will straighten back up again when you let go. But if you bend it until it breaks, it cannot straighten back up. This is a picture of burnout. If we continuously change and change and change, eventually something inside may snap. When this happens, healing comes slowly, and, scarred and weary, we may not ever get back to the same level of enthusiasm and innocence we once enjoyed.

The following are some ways that leaders can control change and blunt stress:

1. **Slow the rate of change.** If your constituents are already stressed out, slow down! Leaders must know the state of their people. They must realistically assess their constituents' needs and abilities. Don't try to push your people faster than they can move.

2. **Change less often.** The more people are required to change, the more stress they will endure. Is the change really necessary? Is it really God's will? Will it really produce the desired results? Change for its own sake is a sure formula for corporate disaster.

3. **Ignore the "band-wagons."** Just because an idea is new, or because "everyone is doing it," does not mean you have to do it! Resist change that is merely for the sakes of novelty or conformity.

4. **Don't change everything at once.** When change is necessary, most people can benefit from having areas of no change where stability and predictability are assured. These "stability zones" will bring corporate security and anchorage.

5. **Build caring networks.** Nurturing friendships will bring strength and affirmation to a changing organization.

6. **Limit the effect of negative people.** Negative people can be draining and greatly increase the stress of change. As much as possible, try to limit their influence in the organization and their exposure to its people.

7. **Identify and reduce additional stressors.** As much as possible, try to limit stress to only what is absolutely necessary.

8. **Encourage your constituents to exercise, eat right, rest and have fun occasionally.** In the midst of difficult organizational change, these can be the first activities to fall by the wayside, but these disciplines must be maintained for the personal health of all concerned.

9. **Rejoice in the Lord! God did not promise us a stress-free life, but He does give us peace and joy in the midst of the storms.** Jesus said, "In this world you will have trouble. But take heart! I have overcome the world" (John 16:33).

Selected Bibliography

Conner, Daryl, R. (1992). *Managing at the Speed of Change: How Resilient Managers Succeed and Prosper Where Others Fail.* New York: Villard Books.

Daft, Richard, L. (1999). *Leadership: Theory and Practice.* Forth Worth, TX: The Dryden Press.

Kotter, John, P. (1996). *Leading Change.* Boston, MA: Harvard Business School Press.

Lewin, Kurt. (1951). *Field Theory in Social Science.* New York: Harper & Row.

Maurer, Rick. (1996). *Beyond the Wall of Resistance: Unconventional Strategies That Build Support For Change.* Austin, TX: Bard Books, Inc.

Rogers, Everett, M. (1995). *Diffusion of Innovations.* 4th ed. New York: The Free Press.

Swenson, Richard, A. (1998). *The Overload Syndrome: Learning To Live Within Your Limits.* Colorado Springs, CO: NavPress.

Woodward, Harry, & Bucholz, Steve. (1987). *Aftershock: Helping People Through Corporate Change.* New York: John Wiley & Sons, Inc.

Yukl, Gary. (1998). *Leadership in Organizations.* 4th ed. Upper Saddle River, NJ: Prentice Hall.

Books in the *SpiritBuilt Leadership* Series
by Malcolm Webber, Ph.D.

1. *Leadership.* Deals with the nature of leadership, servant leadership, and other basic leadership issues.

2. *Healthy Leaders.* Presents a simple but effective model of what constitutes a healthy Christian leader.

3. *Leading.* A study of the practices of exemplary leaders.

4. *Building Leaders.* Leaders build leaders! However, leader development is highly complex and very little understood. This book examines core principles of leader development.

5. *Leaders & Managers.* Deals with the distinctions between leaders and managers. Contains extensive worksheets.

6. *Abusive Leadership.* A must read for all Christian leaders. Reveals the true natures and sources of abusive leadership and servant leadership.

7. *Understanding Change.* Leading change is one of the most difficult leadership responsibilities. It is also one of the most important. This book is an excellent primer that will help you understand resistance to change, the change process and how to help people through change.

8. *Building Teams.* What teams are and how they best work.

9. *Understanding Organizations.* A primer on organizational structure.

10. *Women in Leadership.* A biblical study concerning this very controversial issue.

11. ***Healthy Followers.*** The popular conception that "everything depends on leaders" is not entirely correct. Without thoughtful and active followers, the greatest of leaders will fail. This book studies the characteristics of healthy followers and is also a great resource for team building.

12. ***Listening.*** Listening is one of the most important of all leadership skills. This book studies how we can be better listeners and better leaders.

13. ***Transformational Thinking.*** This book introduces a new model of transformational thinking – of loving God with our minds – that identifies the critical thinking capacities of a healthy Christian leader. In addition, practical ways of nurturing those thinking capacities are described.

Strategic Press
www.StrategicPress.org

Strategic Press is a division of Strategic Global Assistance, Inc.
www.sgai.org

513 S. Main St. Suite 2
Elkhart, IN 46516
U.S.A

+1-844-532-3371 (LEADER-1)